Animal Builders

Jeremy Cherfas

Lerner Publications Company
Minneapolis

Contents

Introduction   3

1 **Animal Skills**   4
   Tools and Raw Materials   6

2 **Nest Builders**   8
   Bird Nests   8
   Insect Nests   12
   Mammal Nests   14

3 **Burrows**   16
   Rabbit Behavior   16
   Solitary Mole   17
   Maras   18
   Naked Mole Rats   19

4 **The Master Builder**   20
   The Dam   20
   The Lodge   21
   The Food Store   22
   The Pond   23

5 **Webs and Traps**   24
   The Spider's Web   24

6 **Builders Underwater**   28
   Fish   29
   Water Spiders   29

Glossary   31
Index   31

Introduction

There are many kinds of buildings in the world: houses, offices, stores, and schools. When each is designed, the architect or builder considers the climate, the location, the people who will use it, and the purpose of the building. Will a large family live there? Do the walls need extra protection from the cold? Do the doors need special locks because the neighborhood is not safe?

Throughout the animal world, there are many great builders and types of buildings too. Each is designed according to its purpose, the climate, the location, and the animals' needs. Termites make homes to keep them warm in winter and cool in summer. Spiders build webs to catch insects. Birds build nests in which they raise their young. Beavers build dams and domed houses, with entrance tunnels and storage spaces.

Animals build things for many of the same reasons people do. They build things to help them survive and to protect themselves and their young from heat, cold, rain, and **predators**.

But how does an animal know what and how to build?

Lower left: Termites build towers that look like humans' skyscrapers. This termite mound in Northern Territory, Australia, would be home for several million termites. The nest extends deep into the ground.

Below: The Empire State Building in New York is an example of the skills and techniques of one animal builder: humans.

1 / Animal Skills

Most young animals are born knowing how to make the nests, webs, or other structures they will use as adults. The "blueprints" are built into their brains and nervous systems.

Because the conditions in which animals live can be very different, animals build many different kinds of things. Some are very simple, while others can be quite complicated. Take bird nests, for example. An ostrich has a very simple nest. It lays its eggs out in the open, in a shallow hole scraped out in the ground. But a reed warbler's nest is made out of plant material and is usually well hidden in a bed of reeds.

These two nests are very different because the birds that make them are different and live in different ways. Ostriches live on the open plains of Africa, where they spend most of their time on the ground. Young ostriches can walk and find food soon after they are born. The African plains are warm and sunny. Young ostriches do not need the protection of a nest.

Reed warblers are flying birds that make their homes in dense vegetation near water. Unlike ostriches, young reed warblers are born weak and helpless. They have to stay in the nest for several weeks while their parents bring them food. A sturdy

Ostrich eggs and newly-hatched chicks in the Namibian desert, Africa. The chicks will soon be able to walk away from the nest.

The satin bowerbird lives in northern Australia and New Guinea. The male builds a nest and decorates it to impress a female. Bowerbirds often choose blue objects to decorate the nest.

nest hidden in the reeds provides a safe place where the young birds can develop. It protects the young birds from wind and rain until they have feathers and are strong enough to stand up to the weather. It protects them from predators until they are able to fly to escape.

Like the ostrich and the reed warbler, other kinds of animals build the things that are suited to their particular way of life. Birds are born knowing how to build the same type of nest their parents built, and spiders are born knowing what shape of web to build. Each animal builder inherits this knowledge of the basic blueprint for the structure it builds.

An ostrich may be able to make its simple scraped-out nest correctly on the first try. But a bird that builds a more complex nest may need to begin practicing when it is very young in order to learn to build correctly and quickly. Although an animal knows by **instinct** the pattern of the structure it will build, it often must learn the skills to build the structure correctly.

Male village weaver birds start practicing their nest-building skills when they are very young. As the birds become more experienced, they learn to choose and shape their materials more carefully and weave them together more skillfully into a finished nest.

The reed warbler is a European bird. It builds a nest shaped like a deep cup.

5

Scientists have raised village weavers where they had no grass strips or other suitable nest-weaving material. The birds still tried to "weave" their own feathers or those of their cage mates. At the age of one year, the birds were given their first normal nest materials. It took several months of practice before any of them succeeded in building a nest.

Tools and Raw Materials

The variety of raw materials animals use is just as wide as the variety of structures they build. Scientists used to think that people were the only animals that used tools. Now we know that many other animals make and use tools.

Chimpanzees learn from other chimpanzees how to use a stick or blade of grass as a tool to unearth termites.

Below: Chimpanzees sometimes use flowers or leaves as sponges for carrying water to their mouths, or as rags for cleaning their fur.

The most famous animal tool-makers are probably the African chimpanzees studied by scientist Jane Goodall. Goodall watched chimps carefully break off grass stems and carry them to termite mounds. The chimps poked the stems into holes in the mounds. When the termites grabbed onto the grass stems, the chimps pulled the stems out and sucked the termites off.

Chimps can make other kinds of tools out of leaves. They use handfuls of leaves as sponges to soak up water for drinking. They use sticks to enlarge holes so they can reach honey or tree-dwelling ants. They also use leaves as rags to clean themselves.

Chimps do not use tools to build things, but some other animals do. Digger wasps pick up small stones and use them to pack down the seals over their burrows. A male satin bowerbird often makes a "paintbrush" to decorate his nest. He finds a piece of stringy bark and pecks at it to separate the fibers. Then he mashes a berry to get the juice. He dips the bark into this "paint" and wipes it on the walls of his nest.

Many animals do not need to make tools. They have built-in tools. The mole has strong front paws with which to dig. Beavers cut down trees with their large and powerful teeth. Birds use their bills to weave grass and other materials into nests.

Some animal builders not only have their own tools but also their own factories for making raw materials. The paradise fish blows air and **mucus** into the water to build a nest out of bubbles. Birds known as swiftlets use their **saliva** to make and glue their nests in caves. Stuck to the wall of the cave, the nest hardens into a tiny cup that holds eggs. Bees produce the wax from which they build their honeycombs.

Animal builders use these raw materials and others taken from nature to produce many kinds of remarkable structures. Let's take a closer look at some of them.

Swiftlets are remarkable nest builders. They make cup-shaped nests using saliva from their mouths to cement and harden the nesting material. Swiftlets usually nest in colonies.

Siamese fighting fish come from Malaysia and Thailand. Like paradise fish, they use their saliva to make bubbles. The bubbles cling together to form a nest at the surface of the water.

2 / *Nest Builders*

Bird Nests

Although some birds do not build nests, most do. The most common shape for a nest is probably a deep cup. The nest may rest on the ground in a concealed place or high in a tree. To build a cup nest, a bird gathers twigs and grasses and piles them into a platform. Next the bird presses its body into the top of the platform and turns around and around to create a hollow. At the same time, it thrusts its legs against the twigs to press them closer together. It uses its beak to poke loose ends back into the nest. These actions press and weave the twigs into a strong wall.

When the cup is deep enough, the bird collects soft materials, such as spider web, hair, moss, and feathers. It lines and pads the cup with these soft materials, and the nest is ready for the eggs.

The European song thrush builds a nest of grasses and plant materials. It presses the materials into a cup shape and lines the nest with mud.

Safe and Warm

To protect themselves and their eggs from bad weather or predators, some birds adapt this design. Some wrens, for example, build ball-shaped nests with entrance holes on the sides. The nest is made of leaves and twigs and is well hidden in bushes or tree stumps near the ground. Other birds build their nests at the end of long, slender branches where predators cannot reach them.

The European common wren builds its nest near the ground, concealed in a bush or a tree stump. The nest has a small opening on one side.

Hanging from a branch high above the ground, the nest of the penduline titmouse is safer than that of the wren. Its location and its small entrance help protect the titmouse chicks from predators.

The Penduline Titmouse

The penduline titmouse is a bird of southern Europe and Asia. The male titmouse builds the nest, always at the end of a hanging branch. This titmouse begins by winding blades of grass around a tree branch. Then, using longer blades of grass, the bird weaves a rope that hangs from the branch. The rope is split into two ends, and the bird skillfully weaves a bridge between the two ends. Then the titmouse stands on the bridge and uses its beak to push and pull blades of grass into a ball-shaped nest. The nest's entrance hole is on its side. To make it cozy inside, the titmouse lines it with fluffy seeds.

It has been said that the nest of a penduline titmouse is so well built that it is sometimes used as a purse in Africa or as children's slippers in Asia.

Weaver Birds

African weaver birds also make nests at the ends of branches. The male weaver bird builds the nest by weaving a framework with its beak and feet. The entrance is at the bottom, which makes it hard for snakes and other predators to steal the eggs.

Incubator Birds

One remarkable type of nest might not be considered a nest at all. Certain birds in Australia and New Guinea build huge mounds that protect their eggs and keep them warm. They are usually called **incubator** birds, but their scientific family is Megapodiidae, which means "big feet."

Top: A weaver bird begins his nest by twisting a strip of grass around a twig shaped like an upside-down letter Y. He twists long strips of plant matter around the twig and joins them together at the bottom to form a ring. He then stands on the ring to weave his nest. Some weaver birds make a long entrance tube, possibly as protection against snakes.

Left: A golden weaver at the entrance to its nest.

One kind of incubator bird, the mallee fowl, spends 11 months of the year building and maintaining its nest. The male begins by using its big feet to dig a four-foot- (1.2-meter-) deep pit in the ground. Then he collects vegetation, and fills the pit with it. After rain has soaked the mound of vegetation, he covers it with sand.

Sealed off from air under the sand, the vegetation starts to rot and heats up, just like a compost heap. Each day, the male tests the temperature. If it is too hot, he makes little tunnels for ventilation. If it is too cold, he adds more sand. When the female is ready to lay her eggs, the male digs a hole in the mound for her.

The female lays 5 to 35 eggs over a period of several months. Each chick hatches after seven weeks of incubation and digs out of the mound to freedom. The chicks fly away as soon as they are able, perhaps a day after they come out of the mound. They never meet their parents.

Mallee fowls use their large feet to build and tend incubator mounds for their eggs. The birds are able to keep the temperature of the mound very stable by adding or scratching away sand.

Insect Nests

The names of the carpenter ant, mason bee, and potter wasp roughly describe what these insects do. They are just a few of the many great insect builders. While insects often work together to make astonishing structures, it is surprising what a single insect can accomplish.

An Insect Potter

The female potter wasp makes her nest alone. She begins by scooping up a ball of clay, which she moistens with water she has drunk. She flies with the clay to a spot she has chosen, usually on a plant. Back and forth she flies, as she gathers clay to build a jug-shaped nest with a narrow neck.

The structure is both a pantry and a nest. The wasp catches caterpillars, stings them to paralyze them, and stuffs them into the pot. Then she lays an egg inside the nest. She seals the pot with a final blob of clay and leaves. A **larva** hatches from the egg, feeds on the caterpillars, and eventually breaks out of its nursery.

The paper wasp builds a nest out of a kind of paper. She chews small pieces of wood into a moist paper pulp and builds her nest from this pulp.

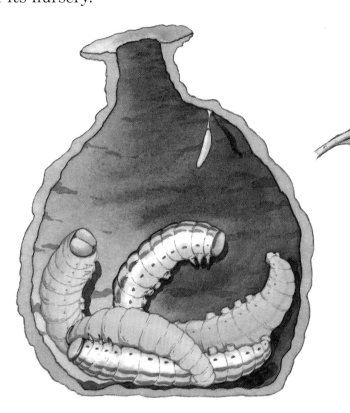

Above: A potter wasp's nest seen from the outside. Left: A potter wasp's nest sliced down the middle would look like this. The single egg is hanging by a thread from the top of the nest.

The cells of a honeycomb have several uses. Some cells contain honey for workers to feed on. Other cells are used to store honey for the winter or as brood cells for young bees.

Below: Several honeycombs of wild bees. As the number of bees in a colony grows, the worker bees build new combs. Each honeycomb contains hundreds of cells.

The Precise Honeybee

Honeybees build their nests in hollow trees or in the hives that a beekeeper provides. The nests, called honeycombs, are made from wax produced by female bees. A honeycomb is made up of six-sided cells. In some cells, the queen bee lays eggs. In others, worker bees store honey and pollen.

A bee produces wax in special **glands**. The wax oozes through the bee's body onto its abdomen, and the bee then picks it off with its legs. She chews and mixes the wax with saliva until it is smooth and soft. Then she adds the wax to the honeycomb.

Bees work very well together and are remarkably efficient. No wax is wasted, and all of the cells fit very neatly together. When building the honeycomb, the workers form a column between the honeycomb and the frame or surface below. They actually hang on to one another to support the bees at work and the developing honeycomb.

Mammal Nests

Not many **mammals** build nests. It is usually the smaller mammals, such as **rodents**, that build nests. The mammals that do build nests, however, may be as skillful as any bird. The harvest mouse, for example, weaves a warm nest of grass among stalks of wheat or barley.

Pack Rats and Squirrels

In North America there are animals called pack rats that build huge, untidy nests. They live in mountain or desert areas and build nests of sticks, twigs, cactus, and even bones. The nest pile is often more than three feet (one meter) high. Inside there are several rooms—a sleeping area, a nursery, a pantry for storing food, and a toilet. Pack rats are curious about everything around them and like shiny things. They carry to their nests items such as bits of metal or glass, nails, or brightly colored stones.

The European dormouse is a rodent. It builds a ball-shaped nest with an entrance hole on the side, similar to the nests of some mice.

The pack rat or wood rat builds a large, untidy mound. It makes a home of several rooms beneath this mound.

Squirrels also collect sticks and twigs to form a nest. The nest is wedged between branches near the trunk of the tree. The squirrels build their nests in summer and autumn, hibernate in them during the winter, and bear their young in them in spring.

The Big and the Small

Along the coast of Kenya, in East Africa, lives a small animal called the golden-rumped elephant shrew. It usually sleeps under a pile of leaves. This messy covering conceals a hollow in the ground lined with soft material.

Two elephant shrews may share a **territory**, but they sleep in separate nests. They often have many nests scattered around and use a different one each night. In this way, they avoid predators that might wait for them at their nest at night.

While most mammals that build nests are small, some big mammals build nests too. Gorillas and chimpanzees make a rough bed for themselves out of plants and branches. Mountain gorillas make a new nest on the ground each night, and any time they stop for a rest and a snooze during the day. Chimpanzees usually make their beds in trees.

The elephant shrew of Kenya is named for its long, trunk-like snout.

This mountain gorilla has made a nest for its midday nap by bending twigs and branches down and in to make a bed.

3 / Burrows

Many animals will use a crack between two rocks or a hole in the ground to hide in. Other animals build large dens or dig elaborate burrows, complete with shafts for air and chambers for sleeping, feeding, and hiding from danger. Some animals work alone on construction, while others, such as the prairie dog, work in teams.

Rabbit Behavior

The common rabbit of Europe lives in fields or on hills in a **colony** called a "warren." A warren is a complicated set of burrows, which the members of a colony share. There are many entrances and hidden exits, and nesting dens off the main tunnels. Burrows built in hard ground last a long time. Rabbits often take over abandoned burrows rather than working to dig new ones. Female rabbits, called does, will fight to win a burrow. Out at the warren's edge, there is more danger from predators. The younger or less powerful rabbits will be left to the dens at the edges of the colony's warren.

In softer ground, such as sand dunes, the female rabbits dig their own burrows far apart from each

European rabbits live in underground colonies to protect themselves from their many enemies. This drawing of a rabbit warren shows an entrance, nesting den, and some of the many tunnels and rooms that may make up a warren. A rabbit warren may last for tens or hundreds of years.

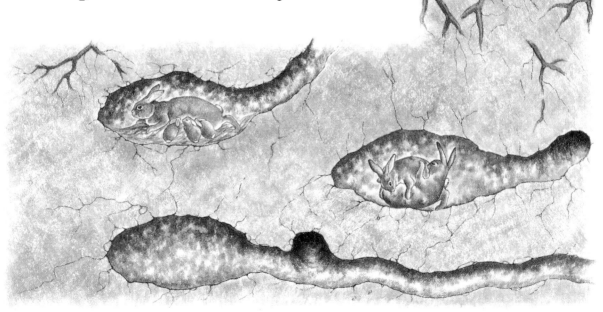

Left: The powerful front paws of a mole are turned outward for ease in burrowing.

Above: Every so often as they dig, moles have to remove the loose soil from their tunnels. This extra soil is shovelled to the surface, making molehills such as the ones in this English field.

other. They may have to dig new burrows often because burrows in soft ground collapse easily. The rabbits seldom fight over burrows dug in softer ground.

Solitary Mole

Moles live under the ground and are very solitary. They know the locations of neighboring moles' burrows and avoid them. If a mole should die, however, its burrows will be taken over very quickly. Moles can dig with their powerful front paws for hundreds of feet, without stopping. The paws are broad, like shovels, with five strong claws that loosen the soil like a fork. When the mole digs deep tunnels, it uses its front paws to push the loose soil into a pile. A "molehill" forms when a mole pushes the loosened soil upward to the surface of the ground.

Moles have an extensive burrow system with a central chamber, a nest chamber, and other small rooms. The many tunnels are used for safety and as traps for food. The mole eats earthworms and other creatures, such as snakes and mice, that have fallen through the roof of the tunnel.

Maras

The mara, a long-legged rodent of South America, digs a burrow for its young to protect them. Maras live in pairs in their own territory, except during the breeding season, when many pairs get together and dig a large den. The females give birth outside the den, and the young crawl inside. The mother returns to the den twice a day to feed her young. While she feeds the pups, her mate stands guard. A pair of maras is almost always at the den, and thereby the young are further protected.

These mara pups sit outside their communal burrow. The young shown here belong to at least six different pairs of parents.

Naked Mole Rats

One of the biggest burrows of all is made by a small rodent called the naked mole rat. It lives in East Africa, where it uses its sharp teeth to gnaw through soil that can be as hard as concrete. Naked mole rats live in large colonies. Like bees, only one female breeds and rules the colony as a single queen. All of her offspring are workers who dig the tunnel system and gather food.

Naked mole rats are blind with skin covering their tiny eyes. They are naked because they do not need fur to keep warm. The temperature in their tunnels is always comfortable, even if it's very hot or cold above ground.

The naked mole rat of Africa is almost entirely hairless. It is more closely related to a rat than to a mole. It uses its front teeth rather than specialized front paws for burrowing.

A Chain Gang

Mole rats set up a chain gang to tunnel through soil. One animal works at the front, biting into the dirt. It kicks the soil into the face of the one behind it. Each animal kicks the soil back, until the dirt reaches the mole rat near the surface, who flings it out onto the ground. An active hole looks like a volcano, with puffs of dirt coming out.

As they dig, the mole rats search for bulbs and roots to eat. They live in a hot, dry semi-desert, where food is scarce. One animal alone could never dig far enough to find enough to eat. A colony working together, however, can find food enough for all of them. The mole rats' tunnels can be up to two miles long.

4 / *The Master Builder*

It is almost impossible to single out one animal as the best builder of all. But the beaver, because of the many different structures it builds and its remarkable skill in building them, is exceptional.

Beavers live in family groups. Older offspring stay with their parents, and all except the youngest, the kits, work on the various construction projects, such as cutting trees, damming streams, and digging canals.

The Dam

If beavers live on a large lake, they may not bother to build a dam. But if they live on a stream, they will create a lake by blocking the stream with a dam of sticks, stones, and mud.

Once the beavers have chosen a site for the dam, they cut down large trees nearby. Using its huge front teeth as an ax, a beaver can chop down a tree more than one foot (30 cm) in diameter. Beavers' teeth continue to grow all their lives, and a lifetime of chewing keeps the teeth sharp.

Beavers begin the dam's construction by placing one of the fallen trees across the stream and wedging its end against other trees or rocks on the bank. The beavers then pile short thick logs against the fallen tree so that it forms a wall. Smaller sticks and mud are used to make the dam stronger and plug holes. The dam creates a pool on one side, in which the beavers build their lodge.

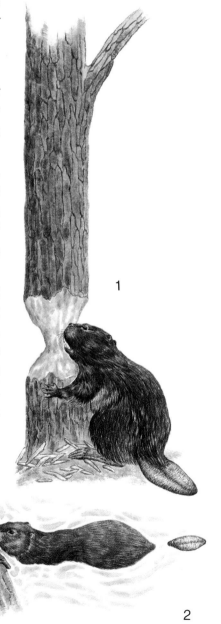

Beavers fell a few large trees. Bottom: A beaver pushes a log across the stream to add to the dam.
Lower left: Then it piles small branches onto the log and plasters them down with more mud.

1

3

2

The Lodge

In the pool created by the dam, the beavers build a lodge on the riverbank or pond floor. The lodge is a domed structure of woven sticks and mud. The living area is the inside chamber of the dome and is always above water. Here the beavers sleep and feed their young. An entrance tunnel extends from the living area to somewhere underwater.

Because of the dam, the water surrounding the lodge rises. The beavers must work constantly to keep their living area above water.

They raise the floor by adding fresh mud and raise the ceiling by scraping mud away. Then they pile

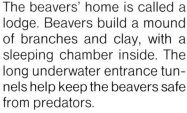

The beavers' home is called a lodge. Beavers build a mound of branches and clay, with a sleeping chamber inside. The long underwater entrance tunnels help keep the beavers safe from predators.

This is what a beaver lodge looks like from the outside.

more sticks and mud on the outside to strengthen the roof.

Sometimes the water level rises so the lodge is completely surrounded by water, making the beavers completely safe from predators.

The Food Store

Beavers eat the leaves and bark from branches and slender trees. In the summer, when the trees are in leaf and the bark is green and full of sap, finding food is no problem. But what do they eat in the winter?

One purpose of the dam is to make the pond deep enough so the water at the bottom does not freeze in winter. In the summer and fall, beavers collect many more twigs and branches than they normally eat. They store these under water near the lodge, holding them down with stones and mud. The cold water keeps the food fresh. All winter, the beavers can leave their lodge through the underwater entrance and get food they have stored.

If the beavers use up all the trees around the edge of their pond, they will need to go farther afield. Since the felled trees are large and heavy, the beavers may not be able to drag them the entire distance. Therefore, the beavers dig ditches in the soft mud from the trees to the pond. The ditch fills with water, making a canal, and the beavers float the logs to their pond.

Beavers make underwater stockpiles of branches and slender trees. They weigh these down with stones and use them as a food store for the winter months.

Beavers are well equipped for life on land and in water. Their back feet are webbed, as shown here, and help them swim. Their front feet are not webbed and work almost like hands.

The Pond

The pond formed by the dam greatly affects the surrounding environment. Silt and mud carried down by the stream form a boggy marsh around the pond. This marsh is where the beavers' favorite food, alder and willow trees, grows best. So you could say that beavers are farmers as well as builders.

People object when the beavers flood cropland or highways, or cut down the trees in their yard. But the beavers make a place suitable for all kinds of wildlife—including themselves. From mosquitos to moose, many types of animals are drawn to beaver ponds to eat, drink, and live.

Beavers build a dam so the top is above the water. Whenever a leak or break occurs, they work quickly to repair it. Beavers may keep their dam in good condition for years.

5 / Webs and Traps

Many animals lie in wait to ambush their food. Some build a trap. The ant lion, for example, uses a trap to capture ants.

The ant lion is the larva of an insect similar to a mayfly. To catch ants, it digs a pit in sandy soil with its enormous pincer-shaped jaws and lies in the bottom. An ant that stumbles into the pit slides to the bottom and into the jaws of the ant lion. If the ant seems to be escaping, the ant lion knocks it off balance by pulling away the sand under its feet.

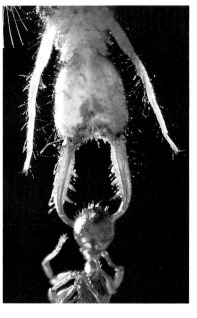

Above: An ant held in the jaws of an ant lion.
Left: This drawing shows the funnel-shaped trap an ant lion builds, with the ant lion waiting at the bottom.

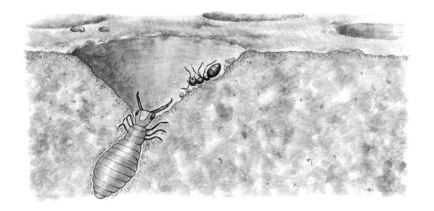

The Spider's Web

The best-known animal trap is the spider's web. Spiders build with two kinds of silk, dry threads for basic building, and sticky threads for the trap. Both kinds of silk are made in glands in the spider's abdomen. All spiders can make silk, but not all of them build the elaborate traps called orb webs.

The trap-door spider digs a burrow in which it hides. The spider weaves a lid of silk for the burrow, attaching it with a hinge of silk. This is the trap door, from which the spider takes its name. When a small insect walks by, the spider feels the vibrations of its footsteps. Then it rushes out and attacks the **prey.**

A trap-door spider about to enter its burrow. The trap-door lid is at the bottom of the picture.

24

An orb web is easiest to see when it's covered with early-morning dew. Early morning is the best time to find webs and study how they are made.

Making the Web

Orb webs are a masterpiece of building. To begin the web, the spider sits on a branch or rock, and lets out a fine thread of dry silk. The end of the thread floats away until it snags on another object, such as a tree, and becomes a bridge. If the line does not catch on anything, the spider hauls it in, eating the silk as it is reeled in. Then the spider tries again, until it has formed the bridge. The spider walks across the bridge and lets out a heavier thread to reinforce it.

To build a frame for the web, the spider forms threads and attaches them at both ends of the bridge. Then it moves to the center, where it allows itself to drop down. This forms a Y-shaped thread hanging from the bridge. The spider attaches the bottom of the Y to an object or surface below.

The spider climbs the spokes of the Y and makes an outside frame and more spokes from the center. The center of the Y will be the hub of the web, where the spider sits and waits for prey.

Once the spokes are in place, the spider lets out a dry thread as it moves in a spiral. This is not the trap, but a scaffold or platform. When the spider finishes the scaffold, it retraces its steps, letting out a sticky thread. The spider eats the scaffolding as it goes. By eating the silk, the spider recycles the protein used to make the silk.

Trapping a Meal

The spider sits at the hub, with each of its eight legs on one of the spokes. When an insect is snagged in the web, the spider feels the vibrations of its struggle. From the vibration, it knows the size and location of the prey. The spider then rushes over to it. If the insect is too big, the spider cuts it loose before it damages the web. Otherwise, it grabs the prey and bites it, injecting a poison to paralyze it. Then it wraps up the prey and carries it back to the hub.

The spider may eat its prey immediately. If it is not hungry, the spider attaches a thread to the wrapped food package and hangs it beneath the web for later.

This *Argiope* spider has trapped a butterfly in its orb web. The spider is wrapping it up in silk as a meal for the future.

These tent caterpillars spin silk much like spiders do. They build a silken "tent" that they use as a home.

Snare Ropes and Nets

The bolas spider spins a single thread with a sticky drop at the end. The spider whirls the thread around to catch insects. The spider's name comes from the similar snare rope, the *bolas,* used by Argentinian cowboys.

Dinopis, another spider, builds a small web and snips it free of the support lines. The spider hangs by a thread close to the ground and holds the web like a net in its front legs. When an insect comes near, the spider throws its net to catch the prey.

The *Dinopis* spider holds its net ready to throw over a passing insect.

6 / *Builders Underwater*

Coral is a home made by tiny soft-bodied animals called polyps. Each polyp builds its own limestone house. Though each polyp is barely the size of a pea, a colony of polyps together builds an enormous house. These colonies are called coral reefs.

Coral is the polyp's limestone skeleton, which the animal makes to support and protect itself. Over millions of years, as generations of polyps build their homes, reproduce, and die, their skeletons can form massive structures. Often, the coral forms a fringe around an island, or becomes a reef along the coast, like the Great Barrier Reef of Australia.

Above: In many tropical waters, coral provides beautiful underwater scenery.

Seen from the air at low tide, part of the Great Barrier Reef of Australia. Over many years, a reef such as this may be built up above the water's surface.

Fish

Other underwater builders live on the reef. Each night the parrotfish spits out a covering of mucus in which it sleeps. This sleeping bag protects it from predators. Some underwater worms build hard tubes in which to live.

The well-digger jawfish of Southeast Asia digs a vertical tube in the seabed by using its large jaws to remove mouthfuls of sand. It collects stones and bits of shell and presses them into the wall of the well to hold it together. The fish hides in its hole most of the time. When it needs to eat, the fish comes out and lies quietly on the seabed nearby. Its large jaws are as useful for catching food as for digging a well. If a bigger fish threatens, the jawfish scoots back into its hole.

Many fish build nests to keep their eggs safe from predators. Some use their mouths to excavate a hollow. Others, like the sunfish in North America, use their tails to brush away sand from a spot that will become a nest. Many fish use their saliva to glue together bits of water plants and other debris into a different type of nest.

A trail of mucus is coming out of this parrotfish's mouth. This mucus forms a protecting shroud around the fish while it sleeps.

Water Spiders

Fish have **gills** that allow them to breathe underwater. Spiders do not have gills; they need to breathe air. One **species** of spiders, however, manages to live its entire life underwater.

Underwater, it spins a sheet of fine silk anchored to plants with silken thread. The spider then goes to the surface and traps a bubble of air between its back legs. It swims down under the silken sheet and releases the bubble, which pushes upward. The sheet forms an air sac. After about a dozen trips, the silk has become a miniature diving bell filled with air. Here the spider will feed, mate, and keep its eggs. It will rise to the surface only to capture new bubbles for its diving bell.

This water spider is found in ditches and ponds throughout Europe and Asia. It is taking its prey back to its air bubble, which is the spider's home.

The diving bell spider leaves its home to hunt in the water, but some animals build underwater nets. One kind of caddisfly larva spins a funnel of silk. The water's current causes pieces of food to float into the funnel and down to the larva.

The diving bell spider and the caddisfly larva are only two of the skilled builders found in the animal world. Animals, from tiny insects to huge mammals, use tools or build for a bewildering number of reasons. Observing these animals closely can tell us a great deal about them and the world in which they live.

Glossary

colony: a group of animals of the same species that live together in the same area

gills: breathing organs that extract dissolved oxygen from the water

gland: an organ in the body that takes substances from the blood and transforms them for use. Worker bees have glands that make wax.

incubator: a container that keeps eggs at the proper temperature so they will hatch

instinct: behavior that is inherited rather than learned

larva: insect or animal in an immature stage of development, after hatching and before becoming an adult

mammal: a warm-blooded animal usually covered with fur, whose young are nourished by milk secreted by the mother

mucus: a slimy fluid secreted by an animal

predator: any animal that hunts and eats other animals

prey: animals that are hunted and eaten as food by other animals

rodent: a relatively small mammal with long front teeth used for gnawing

saliva: a clear liquid produced by glands in the mouth that helps eating and digestion

species: a group of animals or plants that have many characteristics in common. Members of one species cannot usually breed with those of another species.

territory: an area of land occupied and guarded by an animal or a group of animals

Index

Pages shown in *italic* type include pictures of the animals.

ant, *24*
ant lion, *24*
Argiope spider, *26*

ball-shaped nest, *9, 14*
beaver, 3, *7, 20-23*
beaver dam, 3, *20*, 21, 22, *23*
beaver lodge, *21-22*
beaver pond, 20-23
bird nests, 3, *4, 5, 6, 7, 8-11*
bolas spider, 27
bubble nest, 7, 30
burrow, *16, 17*, 18, 19

caddisfly larva, 30

carpenter ant, 12
chimpanzee, *6-7*, 15
colony, 7, *13, 16*, 19, *28*
common rabbit, *16*-17
common wren, *9*
coral, *28*
coral reef, 28
cup-shaped nest, 4-5, 7, 8

den. *See* burrow
digger wasp, 7
Dinopis spider, *27*
diving bell spider, *30*
dormouse, *14*

elephant shrew, *15*

fish nest, *7, 29*

golden-rumped elephant shrew, *15*
golden weaver, *10*
Goodall, Jane, 6
Great Barrier Reef, *28*

harvester mouse, 14
honeybee, 7, *13*
honeycomb, 7, *13*

incubator bird, 10-*11*
insect nest, 3, 7, *12-13*, 27

mallee fowl, *11*
mammal nest, *14-15*
mara, *18*

mason bee, 12
materials for building, 6, *7*
mole, 7, *17*, 19
moose, 23
mosquito, 23
mound nest, 10-*11*, *14*
mountain gorilla, *15*
mucus, 7, *29*

naked mole rat, *19*

orb web, 24-*26*
ostrich, *4-5*

pack rat, *14*
pantry, *12*, *13*, 14, *22*, 26
paper wasp, *12*
paradise fish, 7

parrotfish, *29*
penduline titmouse, *9*
polyp, 28
potter wasp, *12*
prairie dog, 16

rabbit. *See* common rabbit
reed warbler, 4-5

saliva, *9*, 29
satin bowerbird, *5*, 7
Siamese fighting fish, 7
silk, 24-27, 30
song thrush, *8*
spider, 3, 5, *24-27*, 30
squirrel, 14

sunfish, 29
swiftlet, 7

tent caterpillar, *27*
termite, 3, 6
termite mound, *3*, 7
trap, *24-26*
trap-door spider, *24*
tunnel, *16*, *17*, 19, *21*, 22

village weaver bird, 5-6

warren, *16*
wax, 7, *13*
weaver bird, 5-6, *10*
web, 3, 4, 5, *24-27*
well-digger jawfish, 29

This edition first published 1991 by Lerner Publications Company
© Text Jollands Editions 1990
© Artwork Cassell Publishers Limited 1990

Library of Congress Cataloging-In-Publication Data
Cherfas, Jeremy.
    Animal builders / Jeremy Cherfas.
      p. cm.—(How animals behave)
    Includes index.
    Summary: Describes the various skills that animals exhibit in building nests, traps, and larders.
    ISBN 0-8225-2255-1
    1. Animal—Habitations—Juvenile literature.
[1. Animals—Habitations. 2. Animals—Habits and behavior.] I. Title. II. Series: Cherfas, Jeremy. How animals behave.
    QL756.C48   1991
    591.56'4—dc20
                        90-13295
                        CIP
                        AC

Acknowledgments
The publishers wish to thank the following photographers and agencies whose photographs appear in this book. The photographs are credited by page number and position on the page (B-bottom, T-top, L-left, R-right):

Heather Angel/Biophotos, 17L. Ardea London Ltd.: Jean-Paul Ferrero, 6T; Jack Bailey, 8; Peter Steyn, 19; Ron and Valerie Taylor, 28T. Bruce Coleman Ltd.: Robert Perron, 3T; Peter Davey, 6B; Jen and Des Bartlett, 4, 11 (both); Jeff Foott, 14B, 27T; Jane Burton, 7B; Gordon Langsbury, 9B; Charlie Ott, 13; H.J. Flugel, 13; R.I.M. Campbell, 15B; Andy Purcell, 17R; Francisco Erice, 18; Hans Reinhard, 21B; Stephen Krasemann, 22B; Leonard Lee Rue, 23; Frieder Sauer, 24T, 30; M.P.L. Fogden, 27B. Frank Lane Picture Agency: L. Robinson, 5B; Toni Angermayer, 15T. Nature Photographers Ltd.: 25; Maurice Walker, 5T; Jeff Watson, 7T; Colin Carver, 9T; R.S. Daniell, 10L; N.A. Callow, 12T; Owen Newman, 14T; Don Smith, 29. NHPA: Anthony Bannister, 26. Planet Earth Pictures: Debbie Perrin, 3B; David Maitland, 24B; Bill Wood, 28B.

Front cover photograph: © Gerry Ellis/Ellis Wildlife Collection

Editorial planning by Jollands Editions
Designed by Alison Anholt-White
Color origination by Golden Cup Printing Co., Hong Kong
Printed in Great Britain by Eagle Colourbooks Ltd.

Bound in the United States of America